Motorcycles zoom on two wheels.
How fast do they go?

Superbikes go super fast. They go 90 miles per hour!

MOTORCYCLES

by Lee Sullivan Hill

L Lerner Publications Company • Minneapolis

To my friend Susan with thanks for all her help and many mugs of coffee.

This book is available in two editions:
Library binding by Lerner Publications Company, a division of Lerner Publishing Group
Soft cover by First Avenue Editions, an imprint of Lerner Publishing Group
241 First Avenue North
Minneapolis, MN 55401 U.S.A.

Website address: www.lernerbooks.com

Library of Congress Cataloging-in-Publication Data

Hill, Lee Sullivan, 1958–
    Motorcycles / by Lee Sullivan Hill.
        p.   cm. — (Pull ahead books)
    Includes index.
    Summary: Introduces the parts and functions of different kinds of motorcycles.
        ISBN-13: 978–0–8225–0695–9 (lib. bdg. : alk. paper)
        ISBN-10: 0–8225–0695–5 (lib. bdg. : alk. paper)
        ISBN-13: 978–0–8225–9924–1 (pbk. : alk. paper)
        ISBN-10: 0–8225–9924–4 (pbk. : alk. paper)
        1. Motorcycles—Juvenile literature. [1. Motorcycles.]
    I. Title. II. Series.
    TL440.15.H55 2004
    629.227'5–dc22   2003015810

Manufactured in the United States of America
2 3 4 5 6 7 — JR — 11 10 09 08 07 06

See the superbike racer lean into the turn? His knee almost touches the ground!

Dirt bikes race through dirt and mud.

Dirt bikes have
bumpy tires.
Bumpy tires grip
the dirt track.

Street bikes are not made for racing.

But street bikes can lead the parade!

A driver controls the motorcycle.

Sometimes there's room for a rider.
Both driver and rider wear helmets.
Helmets protect heads in a crash.

Leather clothes also protect the rider
and driver. Leather won't rip in a fall.

A windshield protects the driver from wind and bugs.

Ready to go?
Almost!
How do you
start this thing?

Just turn a key and push a button.
VROOM! The motorcycle starts.

An engine makes the motorcycle go.

Motorcycles run on gas like a car. The gas tank is above the engine.

The engine turns the rear wheel. The rear wheel moves the motorcycle.

The front wheel
leads the way.
The driver turns
the handlebars
to steer.

The **throttle** is on the handlebars. The throttle controls the engine.

The driver twists the throttle to go fast or slow.

The **brake lever** is on the handlebars too. The driver squeezes the brake lever to slow down and stop.

All done? A kickstand holds up the motorcycle. The motorcycle will be ready for your next trip.

Ready for another ride? **Touring motorcycles** go fast and far.

Touring motorcycles have soft seats.
Soft seats are good for long rides.

Luggage holds food and clothes for the trip. What will you pack?

This rider is ready for her trip. But hey!
Where's the driver?

Facts about Motorcycles

- The first gas-powered motorcycle was built in 1885. It could go only 12 miles per hour.

- The Harley-Davidson Motor Company is the oldest motorcycle maker in the United States. It was founded in 1903 in Milwaukee, Wisconsin.

- The first motorcycle factory was in Munich, Germany. It opened in 1894.

- The fastest racing motorcycles can go nearly 200 miles per hour.

- Some motorcycle riders and drivers wear yellow rain gear called banana suits. The banana suits keep people from getting soaked in wet weather.

Kinds of Motorcycles

street
bike

dirt bike

superbike

touring
bike

Glossary

brake lever: a lever that a driver squeezes to make the brakes slow down the motorcycle

dirt bikes: motorcycles made for driving in dirt and mud

engine: the machine that powers a motorcycle. Most motorcycle engines run on gas.

street bikes: motorcycles that are built for driving on streets and highways

superbikes: super fast racing motorcycles

throttle: the part that controls the engine and makes the motorcycle go faster or slower

touring motorcycles: motorcycles that are built for long rides. Touring motorcycles usually have soft seats and luggage.

Index

About the Author

Lee Sullivan Hill watches motorcycles zoom by her on the curvy streets of Clarendon Hills, Illinois, and dreams of the day she'll get her own bike—a retro street bike loaded with chrome trim. Lee also loves to ride horses, read, and spend time with her husband and two sons.

Photo Acknowledgments

The photographs in this book are reproduced through the courtesy of: © Sport the Library/SportsChrome USA, pp. 3, 4, 5, 31; © B. Dodge/Photo Network, p. 6; © Todd Strand/Independent Picture Service, pp. 7, 16–20, 22, 23, 25, 26; Wernher Krutein/photovault.com, pp. 8, 10; © Photo Network, p. 9; PhotoDisc Royalty Free by Getty Images, p.11; © Mark E. Gibson/The Image Finders, p. 12; © G. Hofstetter/Photo Network, p. 13; © Robert W. Ginn/Photo Network, p. 14; © Richard Chenet/Transtock, p. 15; Corbis Royalty Free, p. 21; © Dennis Junor/Photo Network, p. 24; © Laura Warfield/Photo Network, p. 27.

Front cover: © Sport the Library/SportsChrome USA